Charlotte Vdovychenko

What's that.....
Banana?

No, they are
Plantains

To order additional copies of this book, contact:
Xlibris
844-714-8691
www.Xlibris.com
Orders@Xlibris.com

ISBN: Softcover   978-1-6698-0158-0
        EBook   978-1-6698-0157-3

Print information available on the last page

Rev. date: 12/07/2021

This book is dedicated to Dr. Kwajo Fordjour, who after studying medicine in Russia during the 60's, returned to practice in Ghana. Unfortunately, he was diagnosed with diabetes in his 50's. He managed his disease with boiled green plantains and spinach stew. I'm glad to say Dr. Fordjour lived over 25yrs after the onset of his illness. I can't say he lived long due to the plantains and spinach, but I would like to say, it helped. Especially, in a culture that knew very little, then, about the disease, and had limited medical and dietary ability in maintaining a healthy diet toward healing.

Why I Found It Necessary to Write This Book

WHILE THIS SUPERFOOD IS POPULAR IN AFRICA, ASIA AND LATAIN AMERICA, IT'S A MYSTERY TO MOST EUROPEANS AND NORTH AMERICANS. PEOPLE USUALLY ASKED ME, AT THE SUPERMARKET, IN MY ADOPTIVE HOME DALLAS TEXAS "WHAT'S THAT BANANA?" I THEN EXPLAIN THE NATURE OF PLANTAIN, HOW IT'S COOKED, AND IT'S NUTRITONAL VALUE.

So, What Are Plantains?

THEY ARE FRUITS THAT ARE USUALLY COOKED AS VEGETABLES. YOU DON'T PEEL THEM AND EAT STRAIGHT LIKE YOU WOULD WITH BANANAS.

MOST CULTURES ENJOY PLANTAINS WITH BEANS STEW, BUT AS YOU WILL SOON FIND OUT, YOU CAN COOK THEM IN MANY DIFFERENT WAYS. YOU MAY HAVE SEEN PLANTAINS SERVED FAMOUSLY AS A SIDE WITH RICE DISHES.

Nutrition:

PLANTAINS ARE VERY RICH IN POTASSIUM, WHICH HELPS CONTROL HEART RATE AND BLOOD PRESSURE. THE HIGH FIBER CONTENT HELPS LOWER CHOLESTROL AS WELL.
(WWW.HEALTHLINE.COM).

POTASSIUM 893MG 25%

VITAMIN C 54%, VITAMIN B-6 25%, MAGNESIUM 16%, AND IRON 6% WITH A DIETARY FIBER OF 16% (USDA)

PLANTIANS CONTAIN ANTI-INFLAMATORY FLAVONOIDS, ANTIMICROBIAL ACTION DUE TO IRIDOID GLYCOSIDE AND TANNINS. ANTIHEMOHAGIC AND EXPECTORANTS ARE QUALITIES OF THIS PLANT AS WELL.
(WWW.HEALTHLINE.COM).

How Do You Cook Plantains!

HERE ARE SOME EXAMPLES OF WAYS TO COOK PLANTAINS:

BECAUSE PLANTAINS ARE EDIBLE AT ANY STAGE OF RIPENESS, THERE ARE MANY WAYS TO COOK THEM. THERE IS NEVER A WASTE WITH THIS PLANT!

PLEASE NOTE THAT IT IS VERY IMPORTANT TO PAY ATTENTION TO WHAT TYPE OF PLANTAIN RIPENESS IS REQUIRED FOR THE RECIPE.

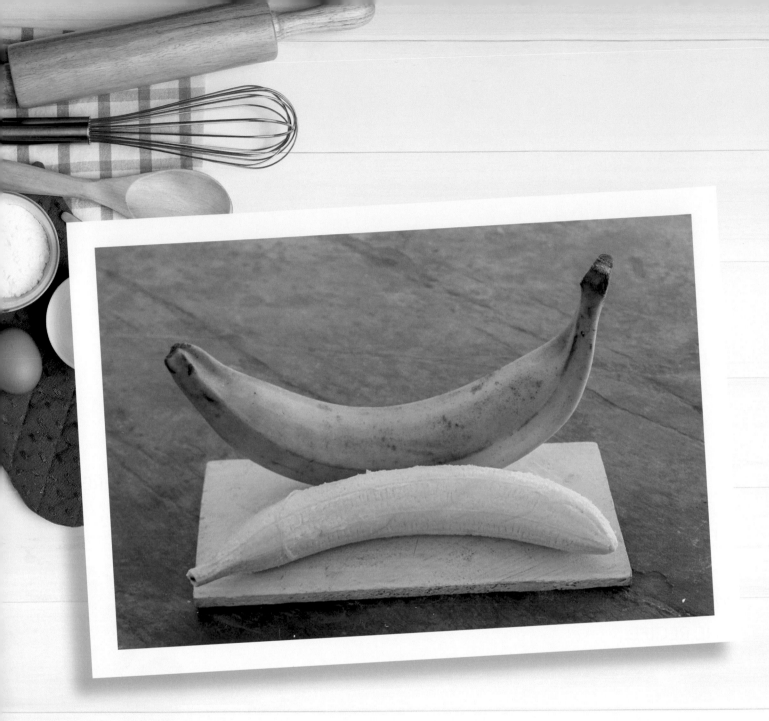

When Green

YOU CAN MAKE PLANTAIN CHIPS, OR BOIL AND EAT WITH ANY SAUCE OF YOUR CHOICE. MASHED OR POUND WITH SOUP OR STEW IS ANOTHER OPTION.

Chips

Mashed

Boil With Omelette

WHEN THEY TURN YELLOW, YOU CAN BOIL, MASH, FRY OR BAKE & ROAST.
EAT WITH SOUP AS WELL AS STEW OR JUST BY ITSELF.

Fried And Served As A Side

WHEN OVERRIPE AND SKIN TURNS BLACK, THIS IS
WHEN IT CARAMELISE, SO YOU CAN TURN THEM INTO
THOSE DELICIOUS SPICY FRITTERS AND DESSERTS.

Over ripped and caramelized

Plantain Crepes Or Pancake Made With Coconut And Raisin.

Aborrajados

(FRIED SWEET PLANTAINS WITH CHEESE: COLOMBIAN TREAT. CAN BE SAVORY AND SWEET AND SERVED AS APPETIZER AND OR DESSERT

Kelewele

GHANA

Spicey Caramerised Fritters.

Fritters & Chips

Fried Plantains Usual Served As A Side.

IT CAN BE EATEN WITH ROASTED PEANUT, OR BY ITSELF.

Kelewele (Fritters)

GHANA's FAMOUS STREET FOOD
SPICEY AND DELICIOUS:

BY CHARLOTTE VDOVYCHENKO
Let This Be Your New Party Favorite!

A favorite evening snack by street vendors. The aroma of the spices brings people from their homes to buy them wrapped in paper. Like chips you can't stop at one bite! Enjoy!!

INGREDIENTS: Over ripped spicy plantains (Ghana kelewale)

3 over riped plantains

A thumb size fresh ginger(grated)

Half a clove of fresh garlic(grated)

Half teasp of salt

Half teasp of black pepper

Half teasp of Anise seeds

Half teasp of Cardamom

Half teasp of cloves

Tblsp of crushed red pepper

2 tbsp planters salted peanuts (if you're allergic) substitute with ground cinnamon.

Peel the over riped plantains and slit them in half. Dice plantains further as shown.

Add all other ingredients to the plantains and fry in hot oil. Avoid turning for the first 5min to keep spices on plantain, and not lose in oil. Only turn Plantains over, in one lump, once one side is golden brown. You can check by flipping one bite by the edge of the flying pan.

When both sides are golden brown place on a plate and sprinkle peanut on it. Substitute peanuts with cinnamon if desired. (recipe By Charlotte Vdovychenko).

TESTONES FROM LATIN AMERICA WILL VERY WELL DELIGHT YOUR GUEST

Riped Fried Plantain

Plantain Puff Puff – Sweet and Spicy (NIGERIAN)

Tostones are crush fried green plantain, with a cup form, in this case filled with a fresh octopus spatter. CANASTICAS DE PLATANO BY ROSA MARIA

ABORRAJADOS (FRIED SWEET PLANTAINS WITH CHEESE:
COLOMBIAN TREAT. CAN BE SAVORY AND SWEET
AND SERVED AS APPETIZER AND OR DESSERT

Nigerian Plantain Chips-Home Made

STORE BOUGHT CHIPS ARE AVAILBLE IN SPECIALTY STORES:
ASIAN,AFRICAN, CARIBBEAN OR WALMART

ROASTED YELLOW PLANTAIN & ROASTED PEANUTS ARE FAVORITE
SNACKS FOR MANY AFRICAN & LATIN AMERICAN NATIONS

Desserts And Cakes

Aborrajados (Fried Sweet Plantains With Cheese) Colombian treat:
They are both savory and sweet—appetizer and/or dessert

Adobe Stock | #331779620

Stuffed ripe plantain fritters made with steamed and mashed ripe plantain filled with coconut sugar and dry fruits

Sweet fried plantain with condensed milk

Caramel Cinnamon Baked Plantains:

Baked plantain slices covered in cinnamon and palm sugar

Delicate tropic dessert of fried plantain served with
melted dark chocolate and whipped cream

Adobe Stock | #453850454

Kaipola or Plantain Pola

is an authentic North kerala Malabar snack baked without using oven.

Torta de banano con arándanos porcionada

Plantain Cake

Slices of home baked whole wheat ripe plantain cake.
It is also called ripe plantain bread.

Adobe Stock | #421083500

Kai Pola | Ripe Plantain Egg Cake

Fried plantain with cheese striped on top,
South American food

Adobe Stock | #201604939

Home made Plantain Crepes

or pancake with plantain coconut raisins mix in the middle.

Served as sides

Close up of delicious hornado, ecuadorian traditional typical andean food served with corn, potato, sweet plantain, salad, avocado in a white plate over a wooden table.

Adobe Stock | #138232378

jollof rice with chicken and
fried plantain, west african cuisine

Traditional Mexican and Central American breakfast. Black beans and plantain

Vegan Food, Plant-based food. Vegetarian meals.
Healthy Contain Meals

Rice cuban style with egg

Served as one pot dish

Adobe Stock #302836916

Cameroonian Poulet DG

FRIED RIPE PLANTAIN COOKED IN SPICY CHICKEN VEGETABLE STEW

Sliced Puerto Rican pastelon de platano maduro close-up in a baking dish. horizontal

Adobe Stock | #294309016

Cameroonian Kondres

Kondre is one of the two national dishes of Cameroon, consisting of platains, tomatoes, onions, spices, and meat such as goat, chicken, or pork.

Stuffed plantain

FROM LATIN AMERICA

Adobe Stock | #193205705

Served As Mashed

Mashed Plantain

Mofongo mashed plantains, garlic and chicharron served with shrimps and broth close-up on a plate. horizontal, rustic style-PUERTO RICAN AND DOMINICAN REPUBLIC (CHICHARRONES DE CERDO)

Traditional Mofongo with plantains, garlic and chicharron served with meat and broth close-up on a plate. horizontal

Adobe Stock | #415661761

*Meal in Dominican Republic –
fried cheese with mangu (mashed plantains)*

Mashed plantain banana and stomach meat with Puerto Rico flag

Adobe Stock | #356064833

Flank steak with mashed plantain,
collard greens and ginger peanuts

Fufu de platano verde maduro, tacaho, Mofongo, mashed boiled plantains with pork meat, onion. Puerto Rico. Amazonian cuisine, Peru, Cuba

Printed in the United States
by Baker & Taylor Publisher Services